KIDS FOOD!

I like Fajitas
because It has
vegdobls in it
and when you have
fen-shit puting mayornwaise
in and all the veg in
when you eat it go it
tasts deloshas.

COMPILED BY THE
CHILDREN OF

EAST PRESTON INFANT SCHOOL
WEST SUSSEX

Published in the UK by
POWERFRESH Limited
Unit 3, Everdon Park,
Heartlands Business Park,
Daventry
NN11 8YJ

Telephone   01327 871 777
Facsimile   01327 879 222
E Mail info@powerfresh.co.uk

Copyright © 2005 East Preston Infant School
Cover and interior layout by Powerfresh
Cover Illustration Georgia Mays

ISBN   1904967302

Printed in Malta By Gutenberg Press
Powerfresh   September 2005

Forward

What do Infant School children like to eat?

Five years ago, when the school embarked upon a healthy eating strategy, we were told (many many times) that we would never persuade our young children to give up crisps and sugary snacks for their mid-morning break.

It's amazing what can be achieved through peer-pressure and consist ant positive messages.

Healthy eating has become part of the school's culture. Infant children moving on to Junior School have used their influence to introduce a healthy eating scheme there too!

OH, WHAT POWER FROM SUCH SMALL PEOPLE!

With thanks to the 'Friends of East Preston Infant School' who made this book happen and to all the children and their families who contributed their favourite recipes to the book

HAPPY HEALTHY COOKING

Brenda Berridge
Head teacher
East Preston Infant School
West Sussex

SAVOURIES

TUNA PASTA MAIN COURSE

Makes 4-6 Servings

1 Small Onion (Finely Chopped)
5-6 Mushrooms (Sliced)
*½ Courgette (Sliced)
*1 Carrot (Diced)
*3-4 Florets of Broccoli
1 Clove of Garlic (Crushed)
*4 Green Beans (Chopped)
1 Tin of Tuna
1 Tin of Tomatoes
1 Table Spoon of Sun dried Tomato Paste or Sauce (e.g. Sacla)
1 Table Spoon of Olive Oil
2 Large handfuls of the Pasta of your Choice - I use Macaroni or Penne
4 Fluid ounces vegetable stock (Optional)

* Vegetables are optional, use whatever you have in the fridge or what's in season

METHOD

◊   Heat the oil in a large pan and add the onion, cook until tender.
◊   Add the Garlic and cook for a further ½ a minute, then add the Tuna, all the vegetables, Tinned Tomatoes and Sun dried Tomato Paste.
◊   Simmer until all the vegetables are tender (if you need more cooking fluid add a little water or vegetable stock.
◊   Meanwhile heat a pan of water; once boiling add the pasta of your choice and cook for approximately 10-15 minutes.
◊   Once the pasta is cooked, drain and add to the sauce.
◊   Mix well and serve.

I normally portion up the excess pasta and freeze. Perfect if you want a quick and nutritious meal

Tuna Pasta

I Like tuna Pasta because its Nice delicious and healthy

Name: Abigail   AGE: 6

TUNA PASTA BAKE

Serves 4. Ready to serve in approximately 35 minutes

INGREDIENTS

14 oz (400g) penne pasta.
Large tin of tuna in sunflower oil.
6oz (150g) margarine.
10 - 12 oz (240g) mature cheese
3 tablespoons plain flour.
¾ pint full milk

METHOD

◊   Grate cheese prior to cooking
◊   Place a small amount of salt in the saucepan
◊   Add pasta
◊   Add oil from tuna.
◊   Pour on boiling water and cook as per packet instructions.

The sauce should take about 10 minutes

◊   In another saucepan melt margarine, add the flour and blend gradually to form a dough-like consistency.
◊   Add milk gradually until a sauce is formed.
◊   Add a handful of cheese and the tin of tuna.
◊   Stir until tuna is distributed evenly into the sauce.
◊   Pre-heat the grill
◊   Drain pasta and pour back into saucepan.
◊   Add the sauce and mix well.
◊   Place in a large oven-proof dish, sprinkle over the remaining cheese and grill till crispy

daddy's tuna pesta Bake

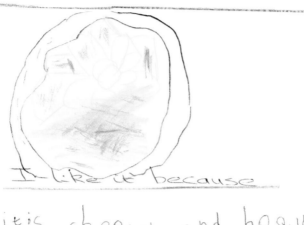

I like it because
it is cheesy and healthy

megan

age 5

COTTAGE PIE

INGREDIENTS

1lb of steak mince
2 heaped tablespoons of gravy granules
7floz boiling water
5 large maris piper potatoes (peeled and cut into small pieces)
1 large knob of butter
Peas and carrots (boil in salted water for 6 minutes)
Slice of tomato to garnish
Grated cheese to garnish

METHOD

◊   Simmer the mince in enough water to cover the mince, stirring until the
     mince is brown.
◊   Drain in a colander (by simmering in the water the fat from the meat can
     easily drained).
◊   Mix the gravy granules with the boiling water and stir into the mince in the
     pan.
◊   Leave to simmer for 20 minutes
◊   Boil the potatoes for 25 minutes and drain.
◊   Return to the pan with a knob of butter and salt and pepper and mash.
◊   Place the mince into a serving dish (warm).
◊   Spoon the potato on top and with a fork cover all the mince.
◊   Sprinkle on grated cheese and garnish with the slice of tomato.
◊   Put under a hot grill to crispen the top.
◊   Serve with peas and carrots.

cottage pie

Louis 6 years old

I like cottage pie becaus
it is yummy and fills me up

FAKES OR GREEK LENTILS

INGREDIENTS

2 cups of brown lentils
1 onion
3 tomatoes
2 tablespoons of vinegar
1 teaspoon of salt

METHOD

◊ Boil lentils for ½ an hour.
◊ Drain water
◊ Chop and saute the onion.
◊ Add lentils.
◊ Chop and add tomatoes.
◊ Add the vinegar and salt
◊ Add 4 cups of water.
◊ Boil for ¾ of an hour and serve

mush bottle

Because the wind[...]

FOUR BIT PIZZA

INGREDIENTS

Dough
4oz margarine
12oz wholemeal flour
½ teaspoon of sea salt
1 tablespoon of olive oil
Cold milk

Toppings
Tomato Puree
Grated Cheese
Mixed herbs
Ham
Pepperoni
Pineapple
Tuna and Sweetcorn

METHOD

◊   Make the dough by rubbing together the flour, margarine and salt.
◊   Add the oil.
◊   Add enough cold milk to make a soft dough
◊   Roll out the dough into three pizzas (or more if you want smaller pizzas).
◊   Put tomato puree onto dough and spread out evenly.
◊   Use a knife to mark the pizza into four sections.
◊   Put separate toppings onto each squares - Ham, pepperoni, Pineapple, Tuna and Sweetcorn.
◊   Cover with grated cheese and herbs.
◊   Cook at Gas Mark 6 (400˚f / 200˚c) for 20 - 30 minutes until cooked.

Four bit pizza

by Luke (7)

It has lots of different things on it and is nice and healthy!

LAURENS CHICK CHICK CHICK CHICK CHICKEN

INGREDIENTS

1 Chicken Breast (fresh)
1-2 Broccoli Spears (fresh)
1 Tomato
1 Portion of peas
1 Carrot
1 Portion of potatoes (boiled)

METHOD

◊   Steam Vegetables.
◊   Cook Chicken in foil in the oven at 190˚.
◊   And boil the potatoes.

Laurens chick chick chck chick
Chicken

I like this dinner because it is yummy and healthy.

Lauren   Age 5½

HADDOCK FISH CAKE
SWEETCORN CARROTS MASH

INGREDIENTS

1 Medium Haddock Fillet
1lb Potatoes
1 Egg
Low Fat Margarine
Parsley
Salt & Pepper
White Bread Crumbs

haddock Fish cake
haddock Firn cake

Sweet corn carrots
sweet corn carrots

x mash
8 mash

CALLUM

age 5

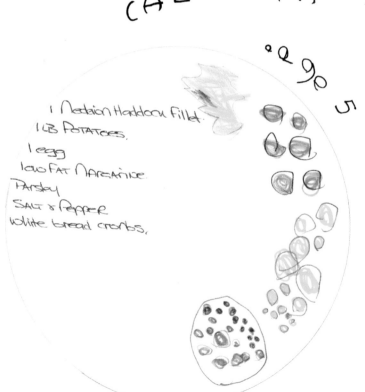

1 Medaion Haddock fillet
1 LB Potatoes.
1 egg
low Fat Margarine
Parsley
Salt & Pepper
White bread crombs.

GARLIC AND GINGER CHICKEN

INGREDIENTS

2 Skinless Chicken Breasts
A Pinch Of Ground Ginger
2 Cloves Of Garlic
A Knob Of Butter
2 Portions Of Rice
Organic Frozen Sweetcorn

METHOD

◊   Cut up the chicken into small pieces.
◊   Peel and cut up the garlic.
◊   Warm Butter in wok and add chicken, garlic and sprinkle over ginger.
◊   Rinse and boil rice.
◊   Boil sweetcorn until soft.
◊   Strain and rinse rice again in boiling water.
◊   When cooked serve chicken on bed of rice with sweetcorn on the side.

garlic and ginger
chicken

I like it because the
chicken is yummitty
scrummitty and the rice
is yummitty as well

Adam 4

19

CHICKEN PIE

INGREDIENTS

Cooked Chicken.
1 Small Tin Of Condensed Soup.
Vegetables - we like to use carrot and sweetcorn
Pastry

METHOD

◊   Pre heat the oven to 180 degrees.
◊   Make the pastry and line a pie dish with pastry and line a pie dish with the pastry - leaving enough pastry to put the lid on the pie.
◊   Put the cooked chicken uncooked vegetables and the tin of condensed soup in a bowl and mix together.
◊   Put the chicken mixture in the pie dish.
◊   Put the lid of pastry on the pie dish.
◊   Brush milk on top of the pie to help it brown.
◊   Cook it in the oven for around 30 minutes
◊   Serve with vegetables and potatoes.

Chicken pie

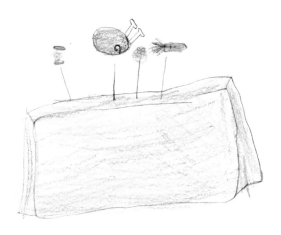

I love the chicken and vegetables — they are yummy

Gemma Age 7yrs

CHICKEN AND SWEET POTATO BALLS

INGREDIENTS

450g Sweet Potato, Peeled & Chopped.
225g Chicken Breast
½-1 Onion.
1 tsp Dried Mixed Herbs — Optional.
1 tbs Milk
White Bread crumbs.

METHOD

◊　Boil potatoes until tender and mash with the milk.
◊　Chop the chicken and onion in a food processor and mix with the potato and herbs.
◊　Form into about 16 balls and coat with bread crumbs..
◊　Saute in sunflower oil until golden.

chicken and sweet potato balls

I like the taske of the
chicken in it.

Bethan   6

Savoury

TOM Penny ages

Pancakes

2 eggs

4oz plain flour

200ml milk

75ml water

2 tbs melted butter

2 oz cheese grated

chopped chives

I like them

because they are yummy

24

Beefy Burgers

1 Red Onion
1lb Minced beef
1 beaten egg
flour for coating
Salt and pepper for seasoning.

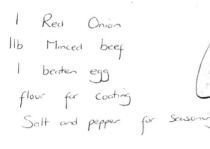

1. Chop onion
2. Mix in minced beef
3. Season with salt and pepper to taste
4. Mix in beaten egg
5. Make into balls and flatten into small rounds.
6. Coat with flour.
7. Grill or shallow fry until golden brown.
8. Serve with freshly prepared salad and new potatoes.

I love these burgers because they are tasty.

FISH PIE

INGREDIENTS

5 Large Potatoes.
100 grams Mature Cheese (Grated).
4 Level Tablespoons of Flour.
4 Frozen Cod Pieces.
1 Pint of Milk.
40 grams of Butter.

METHOD

◊　　Boil, drain and mash potatoes with a bit of milk and butter.
◊　　Cook cod in boiling water until soft, and drain and mash.
◊　　Melt butter in pan, stir in flour and cook for approximately 1 minute.
◊　　Remove the pan from the heat and gradually add milk, stirring all the time until the sauce thickens.
◊　　Add ¾ of the grated cheese, and stir in until smooth.
◊　　Place fish in the bottom of an oven-proof dish.
◊　　Pour the cheese sauce evenly onto the fish.
◊　　Cover the fish and sauce with the mashed potato evenly.
◊　　Sprinkle the remaining cheese over the potato.
◊　　Put into a pre-heated oven at 200°c for approximately 30 minutes or until the top starts to get crispy.
◊　　Serve with either peas and sweetcorn or boiled beans.

Fish Pie

Fish pie

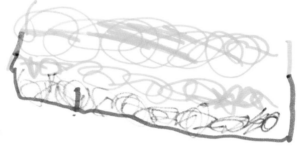

i LiKe Fishpie becAuSe FiSh Fingers hAVe FiSh AndiLiKe fish

5 henry

27

OLIVERS MINCE STEAK BURGER

INGREDIENTS   RECIPE

150 grams of Minced Beef.
1tbsp Of finely chopped Onion.
1 Slice of thin Ham finely chopped.
A little Milk.
Seasoning with Salt and Pepper.
Bread crumbs (Last)

METHOD

◊   Mix it all together add bread crumbs little by little until you get the right consistency.
◊   Shape and fry on the frying pan 4 to 5 minutes on each side in a little olive oil.

INGREDIENTS   POTATOES

METHOD

◊   2 or 3 potatoes sliced, boil and drain them.
◊   Add a little olive oil into a frying pan, when oil is hot, put the potatoes in, seasoning with salt and pepper, fry until nice and crisp.

I like mine served with broccoli and bisto gravy.
It's my favourite dish, because I can help with the mixing and cooking, and it's yummy for my tummy.

My favourite pudding is muller corner crunch.

From Oliver age 6.

oLiver 8906

29

KIDS FAJITAS

Serves 4-6

INGREDIENTS

6 pack Flour Tortillas.
1 Lettuce , sliced
¼−½ Cucumber, sliced.
2-3 Carrots grated.
3 Tomatoes, sliced.
1 Yellow pepper, sliced.
4 Spring onions, chopped.
3oz Cheese, grated.
4 Chicken breasts, sliced.
Mayonnaise, extra light.

METHOD

◊   All ingredients are guidelines only. You may use what suits your family.
◊   Prepare the fillings for your fajitas and place in bowls / small dishes. Give
    everyone a tortilla and let them create their own filling. A really easy, fun
    meal.

KIDS FAJITAS

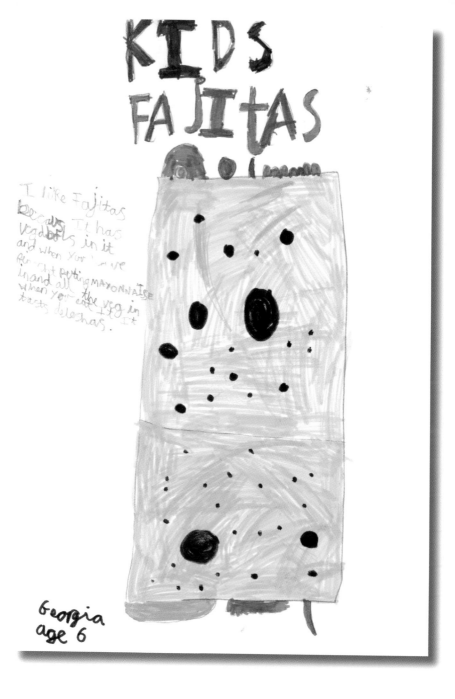

I like fajitas because it has vegdbols in it and when your ave Rememet putting MAYONNAISE in and all the veg in when you eat it it tacts deleshas.

Georgia
age 6

Sea Bream

rub it with salt and pepper and olive oil hten bake it in the oven for 20 minutes.

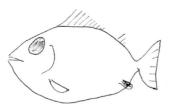

EMILY DUFFIELD

205 of SPaghetti
250g mince
tin tomatoes
ONION
tomato puree

Fry Mince & onion
Add tin of tomatoes & tomato puree
Cook 20 mins.
Cook spaghetti. Then serve.

SPaghetti

Bologhese.

I like it because its yummy

JOShua Gilbing

SPAGHETTI BOLOGNESE

INGREDIENTS

1 Onion
2 Cloves of Garlic
2tbsn Olive Oil
Oregano
1 Oxo Cube
1lb Mince
1 Tin Chopped Tomatoes
Mushrooms
Tomato Puree
Salt & Pepper to taste

METHOD

◊ Heat oil in a frying pan and add the chopped onion and garlic.
◊ Stir for a few minutes before adding the oregano.
◊ Then add the mince and fry until brown.
◊ Now add the Oxo cube and coat the mince before pouring in the chopped tomatoes.
◊ Slice some mushrooms and mix in.
◊ Leave to simmer for about 10 - 15 minutes.
◊ Finally add tomato puree, salt and pepper to taste.

Spaghetti Bolognese

I like slurping pasta

Haedyn   Age 5

SPAGHETTI BOLOGNESE

INGREDIENTS

½pk Whole wheat spaghetti
250g Lean minced beef
1 Large tin of chopped tomatoes
1 Onion, chopped
1 Clove of garlic, crushed
1 Red pepper, chopped
1tbspn Sunflower seeds
1tbspn Pumpkin seeds
2tpsn Beef bovril
1tbspn Sunflower oil

METHOD

◊   Heat water for spaghetti in a large saucepan.
◊   When boiling place spaghetti in water.
◊   Heat sunflower oil in a large frying pan, add onion, garlic and minced beef.
◊   When browned drain fat.
◊   Add the tin of tomatoes, pepper, seeds and bovril.
◊   Stir in well and leave to simmer for about 10 minutes.
◊   Fresh chopped parsley can be added to serve for added colour.

Spaghetti
dolognaise.

H

CRCTTETT TEACT OV YY gee TC

Thea
age 4

37

SPAGHETTI BOLOGNESE

INGREDIENTS

1 Large onion
1 Red onion
5 Carrots
15 Mushrooms
2 Tins of tomatoes
1 Clove of garlic
1 Small glass of red wine
1tbspn Mixed herbs
1tbspn Gravy Granules
1tspn Worcester sauce
Season to taste

METHOD

◊   Put a teaspoon of olive oil in a saucepan and heat up and then place the finely chopped onions in and cook till soft and add seasoning.

◊   Add finely chopped mushrooms and the crushed garlic and red wine. Cook for 5 to 10 minutes.

◊   Add the tinned tomatoes, mixed herbs, Worcester sauce and lastly the carrots and gravy granules. Leave to simmer for 20 minutes stirring occasionally.

◊   Finally add the mince slowly. Leave to cook for a further 45 minutes.

◊   15 minutes before mince finishes cooking, cook the spaghetti.

Spaghetti Bolognaise

chloe age 6

I like this because it is very
tasty and I like sucking it up!
and getting in a mess.

CHICKEN PASTA

INGREDIENTS

1lb Chicken breast fillets
1 Onion (cut into small pieces)
2 Sticks of celery (cut into small pieces)
1 Large carrot (cut into small pieces)
1 Clove of garlic
6oz Sweetcorn
8oz Pasta
¾ pint Cheese sauce
2oz Cheese (grated)

METHOD

◊ Cut the chicken into small pieces and fry in oil until browned.
◊ Add the onion, celery, carrot, garlic and sweetcorn and cook for 20 minutes.
◊ Cook pasta, drain and add to the pan.
◊ Make the cheese sauce and pour into the pan.
◊ Mix well and transfer to an oven proof dish.
◊ Sprinkle the cheese over the top and put under the grill until brown.

Chicken Pasta

I like Chicken Pasta because it is tasty.

Stacey

Age 7

Chicken and Pasta bake
By Lauren Age 6

Ingredients - Serves 4

200g pasta - any shape

2 chicken breasts - cooked & diced

1 can sweetcorn drained

100g brocoli florets - cooked

½ pint white sauce

50g grated cheese (optional)

Cook pasta, drain and put into ovenproof dish add the diced chicken, sweetcorn, brocoli and cover with white sauce. Sprinkle with grated cheese and put into hot oven 200° for about 15 minutes.

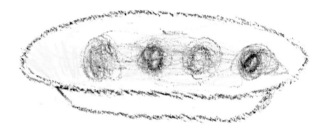

Meatballs in Vegetable Sauce with Spaghetti

Ingredients for the meatballs
2 large handfuls of minced beef (or chicken, lamb)
1 onion – finely chopped
1 clove garlic – finely chopped
1 small handful fresh breadcrumbs
1 tbsp tomato puree
Salt & pepper to season
olive oil to cook

Ingredients for the vegetable sauce
1 onion – chopped
1 courgette – finely chopped
1 red, 1 green pepper – roughly chopped
1 tin chopped tomatoes
1 large handful mushrooms – chopped

To prepare the meatballs – blend all of the ingredients together in large bowl. With a teaspoon, pull off a ball size portion and roll between your palms until compact. Continue until all mixture has been used. Gently heat the oil in a frying pan and cook all the meatballs for about 20mins, turning frequently.

To prepare vegetable sauce – add a little water to a large saucepan and sauté the onions until soft. Add the courgettes and peppers and 1/4pt of water to cook. When softened, add the tinned tomatoes and the mushrooms, bring to the boil and then gently simmer for 15mins. If all vegetables feel tender, remove from heat and blend until it forms a smooth sauce.

To serve – cook spaghetti as per instructions and top with vegetable sauce and meatballs. Sprinkle with Parmesan cheese if desired

Harry loves to slurp the spaghetti!

Harry - Wagtails AGE 5

SAUSAGES IN THEIR BEDS

INGREDIENTS

4oz Flour (4 heaped tablespoons)
1 Egg
1 Cup of milk
Butchers sausages
Veg: Celery, carrots and broccoli or veg of your choice
1 Packet of egg noodles.

METHOD

◊   Set oven (fan assisted) 200°c or adjust to your own oven.
◊   Lightly grease dish.
◊   Mix together flour, egg and milk to form batter mix.
◊   Pour into your dish and then arrange your partly cooked sausages into the
      batter mix.
◊   Place into the centre of the oven for approximately 35 minutes or until
      golden brown.
◊   Serve with steamed celery, broccoli and carrot and noodles, or veg of
      your own choice.

Sausages in Theirbeds

Mix up some batter
Put it in a dish
Put some sausages In the batter
And cook
cook some celory And broccoli
and carrots and put them on
your plate with noodles to
look nice.

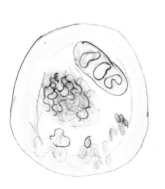

I like it because they are
yummy.

Nathan   age 6

HAM AND BAKED BEAN PIE

METHOD

1   Line a flan dish with short crust pastry
     6oz plain flour and a pinch of salt
     2oz lard or white flora
     ½ - 1oz butter or margarine.
     Small amount of water.

◊   Sieve flour and salt into bowl.
◊   Cut up fats into flour and rub until it looks like fine bread crumbs.
◊   Add about 2floz water slowly, mixing it in with a knife until soft but not sticky.
◊   Kneed lightly and roll out to just bigger than the dish.
◊   Lift and line dish, trimming edges.

2   Make thick parsley sauce
     ½ pint of milk
     ½oz margarine
     1 heaped tablespoon of flour
     2 tablespoons of fresh parsley

◊   Melt butter into a saucepan.
◊   Add four and cook for 1 minute whilst stirring.
◊   Gradually stir in the milk, bringing to boil each time until thick.
◊   Add parsley.

3   Add chopped or minced cooked ham (¾lb) and finely chopped mixed veg if you like into the sauce and pour into lined dish.
     Spread baked beans over the top.

4   Cook for 30 - 40 minutes on gas mark 6 until risen and darkened.

Ham and Baked Bean Pie

mt grandma makes it for me
HOLLY 4 3/4 years old

SCARLETTS GROWING DINNER

INGREDIENTS

Handful of dried pasta (shells / spirals etc.)
4-5 slices of cucumber
1 small tomato - sliced
Handful of garden peas (in pods) - washed and topped and tailed
1 small chicken breast (sliced into goujons)
1 egg
1 tablespoon of milk
Salt and pepper to season
2oz bread crumbs
1 tablespoon sunflower oil / 1oz butter

METHOD

◊   Cut chicken into slices
◊   Mix eggs, milk and salt and pepper in a bowl.
◊   Dip chicken slices into mixture and then roll in bread crumbs until coated.
◊   Heat oil and butter in a frying pan, then add chicken, cook for 5-6 minutes turning until evenly brown.
◊   Cook the dried pasta in boiling water until soft then drain.
◊   Put the cooked chicken and pasta on a plate, arrange vegetables around them and serve.

SCARLETT'S GROWING DINNER

THIS EASTER
NICE AND
MAKES ME
GROW BIG

SCARLETT 4

THAI CHICKEN CURRY

Serves 4-6

INGREDIENTS

500g cubed boneless chicken breast
Thai green curry paste
400ml canned coconut milk
125g pack baby sweetcorn sliced in half
125g pack mange tout

Recipe can be used with any meat, fish, tofu and vegetables.

METHOD

◊ Heat 1 tablespoon of oil in a saucepan and cook 500g of cubed boneless chicken breast for 4-5 minutes until browned.

◊ Add 2-3 tablespoons of curry paste (less for a milder taste) and cook for a further minute.

◊ Add 400ml of coconut milk, bring to boil and simmer over a low to moderate heat for 15-20 minutes, until the sauce has thickened.

◊ 10 minutes before the end add baby sweetcorn, mange tout or any other vegetables such as broccoli or peas.

◊ Serve with fragrant Thai rice cooked as per the packet instructions.

THei CHicKeN
CUrry
LeD Aage 5

I Like THis Recipe
dbecause. it is spicey

51

SHEPHERDS PIE

INGREDIENTS

500g Lamb mince
2 Medium carrots, sliced
100g Peas
100g Sweetcorn
400g can Baked beans
400g can x2 Tinned chopped tomatoes
1 Onion peeled and chopped
25g Wholemeal flour
200ml Lamb stock
1 Bay leaf
Salt and pepper if desired
800g Potatoes, peeled and chopped
60ml Milk
25g Butter or margarine
50g Cheddar cheese, grated

METHOD

◊   Dry fry the lamb mince with the onion, carrots, peas, sweetcorn and bay
    leaf for 8-10 minutes.
◊   Add flour and cook, while stirring for approximately 1 minute. Add the
    tinned tomatoes and stock and cook, while stirring, until the mixture
    thickens. Bring to the boil.
◊   Once boiling, reduce the heat and simmer for approximately 20 minutes.
    Then remove bay leaf and season to taste. Place mixture into oven proof
    casserole dish.
◊   Meanwhile, cook the potatoes in boiling water for approximately 20
    minutes, until well cooked. Drain and mash, adding the butter (or marg)
    and milk and stir well. Spread onto the cooked mixture in casserole dish
    and sprinkle with cheese.
◊   Cook in oven at gas mark 6, 200°c (400°f) for approximately 20 minutes.
    If necessary, place under grill for 2-3 minutes to brown the cheese.
◊   Serve with any green vegetable of your choice.

Mummy'sshepherd's
pie

Finlay
age 5

baked Beans
carrots
tomatoes
peas
sweetcorn
potatoes
onions
lamb mince
cheese

THATCHERS PIE
OUR VERSION OF SHEPHERDS PIE

INGREDIENTS

8oz Realeat vegemince (frozen)
1 Onion
Olive oil
Half a pint of water (add more water if it looks too dry when simmering)
2 tablespoons Worcester sauce
2 teaspoons Mixed herbs
Tin of baked beans
Mashed potato
Grated cheese

METHOD

◊ Chop the onion and fry in some oil.
◊ Add the water, Worcester sauce and herbs and bring to the boil.
◊ Add the vegemince and return to the boil, simmer for 10 minutes.
◊ Place in an oven proof dish, top with baked beans, mashed potato and grated cheese.
◊ Bake in a moderate oven for around 20 minutes until the cheese is melted and golden.
◊ Serve with carrots, peas and sweetcorn.

COLUM 5

CASSEROLE

INGREDIENTS

1lb of stewing steak
2 Onion
½ pint of Guinness
8 Shallots
Potatoes
Carrots
Swede
2 Tablespoons of cereal and pluses (rinsed)
1 Tablespoon of plain flour
2 Oxo
1 Pint of hot water
(Suet and plain flour)

METHOD

◊   Fry the onions and meat in a large saucepan until browned.
◊   Add plain flour, and stir in well, covering all ingredients.
◊   Add shallots, and Guinness and stir for about 10 minutes then add
    vegetables, water and oxo and bring to the boil.
◊   Throw over the cereal and pulses, leave on a very low heat, or in the oven
    at gas mark 2 for 2 hours.
◊   (When cooked, you can add some dumplings to the hot stew, 20 minutes
    before the end of cooking time.)

casserole | Holly
aged 6

Because of the gravy

PASTA AND TOMATO SAUCE

This sauce can also be used on pizza bases and as a base for chicken casserole.
Freezes well

INGREDIENTS

1can Tin tomatoes preferably chopped.
1 Onion finely chopped
1 Clove of garlic (optional)
½ tsp oregano
1 dessert spoon of tomato puree
Grated cheese to garnish

METHOD

◊ Fry the onion and garlic in a small amount of oil.

◊ After a few minutes add the rest of the ingredients. Bring to boil and leave to simmer for about 20 minutes.

◊ Cook your choice of pasta in boiling water. Then serve with sauce on top and some grated cheese.

Pasta

I like this as it tastes nice with cheese on top.

Melissa age 6

59

MACARONI CHEESE BAKE

INGREDIENTS

10oz Short cut macaroni
2oz Butter
2oz Plain flour
1 Pint of milk
8oz Cheddar cheese (grated)
Salt and ground black pepper

METHOD

◊ Pre-heat oven 190°c / 375°f / Gas mark 5. Cook the pasta according to instructions on packet.

◊ Gently melt butter in a saucepan add flour and cook, stirring for 2 minutes. Add the milk a little at a time. Slowly bring to the boil until thickened and cook for 2-3 minutes. Remove the sauce from the heat, season and add 6oz of the grated cheese and stir well.

◊ Drain the pasta and tip into a baking dish. Pour the sauce over the pasta and mix well, then sprinkle remaining cheese over the top. Bake in the oven for 30 minutes until golden brown.

Macaroni Cheese Bake

This is yummy,
with tuna
and swetcorn.

ROSS
age 7

Spanish chiken

copped tin tomato
~~the~~

skinless chiken
mushrooms
red green
~~yell~~ yellow
    peppers
onions
seasoning
chilly and
worcester sauce
tomato pure
surened with
rice

by Rob Hunter

Saskia's super soup

50 g   carrots, peeled and chopped

50 g   leeks, washed and sliced

50 g   potato, peeled and diced.

50 g   split red lentils

600 mls   chicken stock

100 mls   milk

Olive oil for frying

1) Fry the leek in oil gently for
   5 mins, add carrot and potato
   and cook gently for further 5 mins

2) Add stock and lentils and cook/
   simmer for 20mins.

3) Add milk and liquidise

4) Serve with granary bread + butter

Saskia age 5

ANDREWS FISHY DISHY

INGREDIENTS

Fish - Cod, Haddock, Salmon, Prawns (as many as you like)
3 Hard Boiled Eggs
2oz Butter
2oz Plain Flour
Milk (enough to cover and cook the fish in)
Grated cheese
Knob of butter
Mashed potatoes

METHOD

◊ Pour the milk and add a knob of butter in a large saucepan.
◊ Bring to the boil and cook the fish in it for approximately 15 to 20 minutes.
◊ When cooked separate the fish from the skin, remove any bones, flake and place in a large oven proof dish.
◊ Slice the hard boiled eggs and mix with the fish. Then mix in the prawns.
◊ Melt the butter in a saucepan and mix in the flour. When the flour and butter is in a paste gradually mix in the milk (which you strained from cooking the fish in).
◊ Take off the heat and mix in ¾ of the grated cheese.
◊ Pour the sauce over the fish mixture and top with the mashed potato.
◊ Put the remainder of the grated cheese on the top of the potato.
◊ Place in a moderate oven for approximately 30 minutes.

ANDREWS FISH AND DISH

IT IS REALLY
YUMMY AND TASTY

ANDREW   AGE 7

TOBYS LUNCH BOX PASTA

INGREDIENTS

Penne Pasta
Carrot
Cucumber
Cheese
Ham
Sausage (Pepperami or other small sausage)
Mayonnaise - 2 small teaspoons depending on taste.

METHOD

◊ Cook the pasta, drain and leave to go cold. Meanwhile cut the carrot, cucumber and cheese into small pieces and thinly slice the ham and sausage.

◊ When the pasta is cold, separate the pieces and then add the carrot, cucumber, cheese, ham and sausage. Mix the ingredients together and then add the mayonnaise, a little at a time, to combine the ingredients together.

◊ Spoon into individual lunch boxes for a healthy and tasty alternative to sandwiches.

ALTERNATIVE INGREDIENTS

Celery, Peppers, Sweetcorn — according to individual taste.

Tobys Lunch Box
Pasta

I like it because it is
healthy and scrummy and makes
a change from sandwiches
in my Lunch box.

Toby Age 7

PASTA MONTANTE

INGREDIENTS

1 Green Pepper
1 Onion
4 Button Mushrooms
1 Courgette
1 Carrot
1-2tbsp Olive Oil
500g Passata
1tbsp Tomato Puree
½tsp Garlic Granules
1tsp Mixed herbs
Spaghetti / Pasta Quills / Pasta Shells

Serves 4

METHOD

◊ Chop pepper, mushrooms and courgette very finely.
◊ Peel and finely chop onion.
◊ Peel and grate carrot.
◊ Heat olive oil in saucepan and fry vegetables and garlic for a few minutes until softened.
◊ Add passata, tomato puree and mixed herbs.
◊ Bring to the boil, cover and simmer for 30-40 minutes until thickened.
◊ Meanwhile cook pasta in boiling salted water until just soft (about 10 minutes).
◊ Drain pasta and serve with vegetable sauce and top with parmasan cheese.

PASTA MONTANTE

I like this food because it reminds
me of Lady and the Tramp!

Kerensa Age 7

Sammy and George's
age 7   age 5

Healthy Mash Potato

Ingredients: Potatos - peeled
Broccoli - a few spheres
Sweet potato - small piece
Milk and butter for mashing

1 Boil up the potato, sweet potato and broccoli in water
   until soft and drain water away.

2. Mash together, add milk and butter to taste

3. Serve up warm.

Tip - to start with just use small amounts
      of broccoli and increase over time.

" we like it because its creamy and yummy "

SPINACH FISH PIE (serves 4)

1 lb 5 oz skinless smoked haddock fillets	1lb 2oz spinach washed
salt and pepper	1 pint milk
3 oz butter	2 oz plain flour
5 ½ oz cooked prawns	3 tabs chopped parsley
juice of ½ lemon	1 lb 10 ozs potatoes
3 ½ fluid ozs milk	4 ozs grated cheddar cheese

Put spinach into sieve and pour boiling water over to wilt. Squeeze water out.
Arrange at base of casserole dish. Boil potatoes and mash with milk, cheese and
Butter and season. Poach fish in milk for 7 minutes or until opaque. Lift fish out and
drain milk into a jug and keep (for parsley sauce). Make white/parsley sauce, add
lemon juice, fish and prawns to sauce. Spoon fish mixture on top of spinach and
potatoes on the top of the fish mixture. Cut remaining butter into squares and dot
over potato. Bake 30 minutes in over (200 degrees) until golden brown.

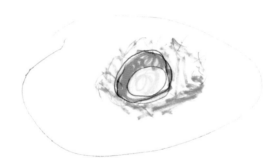

CHICKEN FLAVOURED RICE WITH NOODLES AND CHICKEN

INGREDIENTS

60g of egg noodles
50g of rice (boiled used, but of your choice)
I small carrot
½ small red pepper
1tbsp of sunflower oil
1 small cooked chicken

METHOD

◊   Wash Hands.
◊   Peel small carrot and grate, rinse under cold water and leave covered until required.
◊   Slice pepper into small thin slices, rinse under cold water and leave covered until required.
◊   wash hands and remove skin from chicken , continue to remove chicken breast. Separate into 2 portions, slice portion 1 into slices, use the other portion to dice into small cubes.
◊   Boil a pan of water, once boiling add rice, simmer for 14 minutes and stir occasionally.
◊   While rice is cooking, heat sunflower oil in pan / wok, then add noodles and fry for 5-7 minutes, turn heat down to minimum and stirring occasionally leave to keep warm.
◊   Once rice is cooked rinse with boiling water and drain, then mix with carrot, pepper and chicken cubes.
◊   Serve rice with chicken slices.
◊   Remove noodles from heat and serve immediately.

chicken flavoured rice noodles and
chiken.
I like this because it tastes
nice and Lovely

Chloe age
6

ROAST CHICKEN WITH VEGETABLES

INGREDIENTS

1 Chicken
500g Carrots
Broccoli
Potatoes

METHOD

◊ Pre heat oven to 180°c. Allow 20 minutes per ½ kilo plus 20 minutes for the chicken, and 1 hour for the potatoes.
◊ Place chicken in a roasting dish. Drizzle over some olive oil and sprinkle on some herbs.
◊ Place in the oven
◊ Peel and cut up potatoes, place in a hot roasting pan with olive oil and put in oven, turn every 20 minutes.
◊ Wash and cut up carrots, don't peel them as the skins are full of vitamins. Cook for 20 minutes or until soft.
◊ Drain and place in blender with a knob of butter and some black pepper. Blend for 2 minutes.
◊ Chop up the broccoli and place into boiling water for 6 minutes.
◊ When chicken is cooked leave to stand for 10 minutes and then carve.
◊ Serve with potatoes, carrots and broccoli with gravy if desired.

Roast chicken
with vegetables

warms me up and
makes me run faster

Fraser   Aged   7

NEMO PIE

INGREDIENTS

4 Cod fillets (buy frozen 92g each)
6 Medium size potatoes
1 Onion
Teaspoon of oil
Small tin / frozen sweetcorn
Small tin / frozen peas
2 Tomatoes
Teaspoon of parsley
Pinch of pepper
Cheese sauce ½lb cheese (grated), ½pint milk, tablespoon of cornflour

METHOD

◊   Boil the potatoes for 20 minutes and then mash with a little milk and margarine.
◊   Whilst they are boiling, cook the fish (on HIGH) in the microwave for 2 minutes each or steam for 20 minutes.
◊   Chop the onion and fry in the oil.
◊   Make the cheese sauce by adding cornflour to a little of the milk and mix until it is a smooth paste. Put the rest of the milk into a saucepan until just boiling, add the paste and stir until it thickens then add the grated cheese and stir until melted.
◊   Boil the peas and sweetcorn for about 3 minutes in a saucepan.
◊   When the fish is cooked, mash (removing bones) and add to the onion, peas and sweetcorn and transfer to a large deep oven proof dish. Add the parsley and pepper and mix together.
◊   Pour the cheese sauce over the top and mix in.
◊   Top with the mashed potato and smooth with a fork.
◊   Chop the tomatoes into slices and place on top.
◊   Sprinkle any remaining cheese on top.
◊   Place the dish under a grill until the top goes brown and then serve.

Can be served on its own or with baked beans.

nemo pie

tomato

Choose
fish

Peas

sweetcorn

onion

I like nemo pie

because I like fish

Georg
vitot

FISHY JACKET POTATO

INGREDIENTS

1 Baking potato
1 Tin of sardines in tomato sauce
1 Tablespoon cooked peas
1oz Cheddar cheese grated

METHOD

◊   Pre heat oven to 200˚c.
◊   Wash your potato and prick with a fork.
◊   Bake in the oven for approximately 1 and ½ hours depending on the size of the potato or until cooked through.
◊   Carefully scoop out the middle of the potato into a bowl.
◊   Add the sardines to the bowl and gently mix together with the potato.
◊   Add the peas and combine.
◊   Spoon the mixture back into the potato shells and put in an oven proof dish.
◊   Top with the grated cheese and put under a hot grill to melt.
◊   Serve with a salad garnish.

Fishy Jacket
Potato

Harry age 5

Brandon

TUNÂ or FiSh and white Sauce

TIN TUNA FiSH
LEVAL DESERT SPOON FLOUR
Pieice BUTTER, SALT MILK ½ PINT

MELT BUTTER FLOUR + SALT
STIR TOGETHER WITH MILK TO A SAUCE
ADD TUNA FiSH

PUDDINGS

Lemon Pancakes

4oz plain flour
pinch of salt
pinch of cinnamon
1 beaten egg
$\frac{1}{2}$ pint milk
sugar and lemon to taste
lard for frying.

1. Sieve flour into bowl with a pinch of salt and a pinch of cinnamon.
2. Make a well in the centre.
3. Put beaten egg into the middle.
4. Pour in milk.
5. Whisk until nice and smooth.
6. Put frying pan on heat with melted fat.
7. Pour in batter mix until it covers the bottom of the pan.
8. Cook until the edges turn brown flip over.
9. Put onto heated plate. Sprinkle some sugar and fresh lemon onto pancake.

I love these pancakes because they are sweet and easy to eat.

82

Tropical crunch
Breakfast cereal
is mall lub naturel
yoghurt mixed candied
fruit pineapple ete
dried banana
1 teaspoon cluster
variety cereal
mix all ingredients togethe
in a bou and enioy

LAURENS SWEET STRAWBERRY JELLY

INGREDIENTS

1 pack of strawberry jelly
6-8 strawberries chopped up very small

METHOD

◊ Drop chopped up strawberries into jelly mixture before pouring into mould.

Laurens Sweet Strawberry Jelly

I like this pudding becous it is yummy and
Strawbries are good for me.

Lauren Age 5½

FRUIT ALIEN

INGREDIENTS

½ pint yoghurt (plain flavour)
1oz sugar
2 bananas
8oz strawberries

Toppings
Strawberries
Green grapes
Sultanas
Banana

METHOD

◊   Mash the bananas and strawberries together and add to yoghurt (or blend them together with blender) together with the sugar. Then place into bowls.

◊   Make the alien faces - cut the strawberries into halves and use for ears. Use the halved grapes for eyes with sultanas on top. For the mouth use more sultanas. For nose and ears use slices of banana.

    Sit back and enjoy

Fruit Alien by Luke (7)

I like the fruit alien as each time you make
it he can look different by using different
fruit.

FRUIT KEBABS

INGREDIENTS

Wooden skewers
Bananas, thickly sliced
Strawberries, hulled and halved
Red apples and green apples, cored and chopped
Kiwis, peeled and sliced
Sultanas, peeled and segmented

METHOD

◊   Thread the prepared fruits onto the skewers. (Sometimes it is a good idea to trim the sharp end of the wooden skewers and wrap a little kitchen foil mind each end).

◊   For a special treat add pink and white marshmallows between the fruits.

◊   Serve with some yoghurt.

Fruit kebabs

it is nice, and tasty

ROSS W ALDGE

CHOCOLATE PUDDING

Although not especially healthy, there isn't all the rubbish that you find in shop chocolate puddings.

INGREDIENTS

1 Pint of milk any variety
1½ Tablespoons of cornflour
1 Tablespoon of sugar
1 Tablespoon of Cocoa powder
(If you only have drinking chocolate that's fine but leave out the tablespoon of sugar).

METHOD

◊   Mix cornflour, cocoa and sugar with a little of the milk to form a paste.
◊   Bring the rest of the milk to the boil then add to the paste stirring all the time.
◊   Return to heat and bring back to the boil for a minute or so.
◊   Serve. It's even better with ice cream in the middle.

Chocolate pudding.   Melissa Age 6

I like this as it tastes yummy.

91

JUICE LOLLIES

INGREDIENTS

Fruit Juice - Apple, Orange, Cranberry, Pineapple or any other appealing variety.
Optional Extras - Gummy sweets i.e. : Cola Bottles, Teddy Bears, Jelly Babies,
Jelly tots.

METHOD

◊ You will need a set of loll holders - usually holding 4 lollies. In each
  container place the treat, then add the chosen juice.
◊ Place the sticks on top and freeze until solid. Turn out when ready to eat.

ALTERNATIVE HEALTHY RECIPES

◊ Mix two juices together using the method above.
◊ Layered Chocolate and Banana Angel Delight with Chocolate Buttons.
◊ Strawberry Milkshake Lolly.

Juice Lollies

They taste yummy

Haedyn   Age 5

CakeandCustard

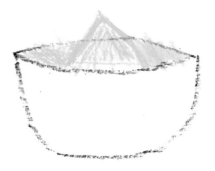

Sponge Cake with Custard

Ingredients:
4oz self-raising flour
4oz margarine
4oz caster sugar
2 eggs
1tsp baking powder
juice of half a lemon

To prepare – blend all of the above ingredients together in a food processor until smooth and creamy. Grease and line 2 x 7inch cake tins and split the mixture between the 2 tins and level with a spatula.
Cook in a preheated oven (170 C) for 25 – 30 mins or until light and golden and spongy to the touch. Cool in tins for 5 mins before turning onto a cooling wire to finish cooling. The 2 cakes can then be sandwiched together using jam.
For pudding – cut a wedge of cake and top with warm custard and serve.
(Harry prefers not to have jam in his cake when he is eating it with custard!!)

Harry - Wagtails Age 5

94

Peach Flan
by Lauren Age 6

Ingredients - Serves 4

1 medium Sponge flan case
1 tin peaches drained
1 orange quick gel
Cream or ice cream

Empty drained peaches onto flan case
Make up quick gel and leave to cool
Slightly then pour over peaches and
leave until set.
Serve with cream or ice cream

PANCAKES WITH STRAWBERRIES

INGREDIENTS

2 teaspoons of icing sugar
125g plain flour
A pinch of salt
1 Egg
½ Pint of milk
Vegetable oil for frying

METHOD

BATTER

◊   Sift flour and salt into bowl with icing sugar.
◊   Make a hole in the middle, add egg, beat well, add milk, mixing with flour from sides until batter smooth.

STRAWBERRIES OR ANY FRUIT LIKE BANANA OR PEAR

◊   Clean, cut up into small chunks, a light dusting of caster sugar might be needed if a little sharp - and leave at room temperature.

◊   Heat oil in frying pan, remove all excess oil.
◊   Pour in thin coat of batter.
◊   Cook for 1-2 minutes until golden brown, turn over and cook other side.

◊   Remove pancake and place on plate. Add strawberries and fold in half, and half again.
◊   Delicious with a little cream too, or ice cream.

pancakes with strawberries

watching MuM cook the pancake
is fun

Holly 4 3/4 years old

Animal Faces.

Ingredients :

Angel Delight or Ice cream

3 or 4 different fruits cut into pieces

In a bowl place your angel delight or Ice cream ,
enough to cover the bottom of the bowl, and then
using your fruit arrange them on top to make a
face , Bear, Lion, Pig, Elephant or even an Owl.

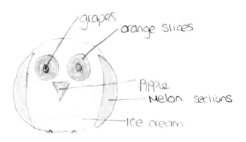

grapes
orange slices
Apple
Melon sections
Ice cream

Nathan age 6.

Animal Faces

They are fun
to make

Nathan age 6

MR HAPPY CHEESECAKE

INGREDIENTS

1 Lemon Jelly
1 Jam Swiss Roll (medium size)
8oz Cream Cheese
3oz Sugar
¼ Pint Sour Cream
5 Strawberries

METHOD

◊　Dissolve jelly in ¼ pint of boiling water.
◊　Arrange ½ inch slices of swiss roll around the sides of a 7" loose base cake tin.
◊　Cut up the remainder of the swiss roll into quarters and put into the base of the tin.
◊　Mix the sugar and cream cheese together and add the sour cream.
◊　When the jelly is beginning to set, add to the mixture and pour into the tin.
◊　Leave to set overnight in the fridge.
◊　When set, loosen tin and place onto large plate.
◊　Cut strawberries into half and place as a smiley face on top of the cheesecake.

Can be served with cream or ice cream.

YUMMY

Cheesecake

strawberry

Swiss roll

I LIke cheesecake

strawberries

George age 4

GRAN'S FLAPJACK

8 ozs margarine (melted)   8 ozs Demerara sugar
11 ozs rolled oats   a pinch of salt
half a jar of mincemeat

Mix all together and press into a tin lined with greaseproof paper (swiss roll tin).
Bake at 350 – 375 degrees for 25 – 30 minutes. Mark our while still warm and cut
when cold.

Trifle

TRIFLE

Packet off Jelly
ANGel delight
TIN of Peaches
SPONGe

Make jelly with half a pint of boiling
water then mix cold water to make
a pint.
Make angel delight, milk + powder
+ whisk.
Put tin of peaches + sponge in trifle
bowl pour over jelly. Let it set in
fridge. Then put angel delight on top.
Decorate if wanted.
IT IS SCRUMMY.

JOSHUA 6

BANOFFEE PIE

INGREDIENTS

Small packet sweet digestive biscuits
1 Tin condensed milk
1 Pot whipping or double cream.
3oz (75g) margarine
3-4 Medium bananas

METHOD

◊ Boil water in a medium to large saucepan, reduce heat and place tin in the saucepan.
◊ Simmer for 2 hours, making sure tin is covered by water for this period.
◊ Melt margarine.
◊ Crush the biscuits and stir into the margarine.
◊ Press into a dish to form base.
◊ Place in fridge until mixture hardens.
◊ Remove tin after approximately 2 hours, taking care when opening (cover with cloth / kitchen roll).
◊ Spread over base.
◊ Leave to cool.
◊ Slice bananas and layer over toffee.
◊ Whip cream until stiff.
◊ Spread over the bananas
◊ Sprinkle with chocolate flake for decoration.

Banoffee pie

I like it because it tastes yummy!

meda h

age 5

Lemon ~~curd~~ curd Steam sprunge Podding

1. ~~Beat~~ ~~3~~ eggs.
2. 6 oz of ~~sugar~~ sugar
3. 6 oz of sr flower
4. 6 oz of butter
5. Put it in a ~~B~~ Bowl and crak the eggs. vnilla.
6. Put I drope of vnilla
~~7. And mix it all together.~~
~~8.~~ Put a little bit of ~~vnilla~~ curd
8. Put spunge mix on top of lemon curd.
9. Cover the ~~stem sprunge~~ ~~pudd~~ Pudding ~~and~~ with tinfoil.
10. Put it in a cooking pot with water.
11. ~~cook~~ Put the pot of mix in the pot ~~with~~ with the water.

12. Put the pot with the mix and water on the cooker and heat the cooker up.
13. When it is fineshed you let it cool down and then you can eat it.

MUESLI BARS

INGREDIENTS

3oz raisins
1oz sunflower seeds
A pinch salt
2tbsp Sesame seeds
3tbsp Warmed honey
3oz oats
1oz cornflakes / rice pops
2 weetabix

METHOD

◊   Oven pre heated to 180°c for 15 minutes
◊   Combine all ingredients together.
◊   Place mixture on a baking tray and flatten down with a spoon (tray needs
     to be greased).
◊   Bake and cut into slices once cooled.

You could melt carob and spread over the top as a substitute for chocolate.

~~Vestt~~ Bars
MUESLi

tothee /

They are
ns and are
healthy.

They are nice and healthy

TOM

7½

Baked Apples

Ingredients

6 cooking apples

75g Demerara sugar

100g dried fruit - sultanas currants raisins or dates

1 tsp cinnamon

75 g soft Brown sugar or 1 tbsp Honey or syrup if preferred.

2 tbsp water.

Method.

cut out the middle of the apples

make a cut around the skin of the apples before placing them in an ovenproof dish ☺

Fill the middle of the apples with the fruit and brown sugar or Honey / syrup. sprinkle the Demerara sugar on top of the apples

Put 2 tbsp of water into the dish and cook the apples for 3/4 Hour — 1 Hour on Gas mark 4

I think that baked Apples taste nice and sweet

By LIAM age 6

baked apples

apple
cook it

its sweet
very very and its
and its healthy
its its nice and
good.

fruit salad
apples
Bananas
pineapple
oranges
orange juicy

its juicy and
its Healthy and its
verey verey good
and its nice

apple pie

Pastre and ~~ff~~

apple
water
flour

Its nice and sweet
its good and healthy
and crunchy

113

GREEK YOGHURT WITH HONEY AND FRUIT PUDDING

INGREDIENTS

Making 1 serving

1 *Small Banana
2 Tablespoons of Greek Yoghurt
1 Teaspoon of Honey
A few Raisins

* You can try using raspberries or strawberries instead of banana and chopped apricots instead of raisins.

METHOD

◊ Slice the banana and place in a serving dish.
◊ Spoon the Greek yoghurt over the banana.
◊ Drizzle the honey over the yoghurt and then sprinkle the raisins on the top.

A quick, simple and delicious recipe.

greek Yogurt and
Honey with Fruit

I Like greek Yogurt and Honey with
Fruit because it is nice and sweet.

Name: Abigail   Age: 6

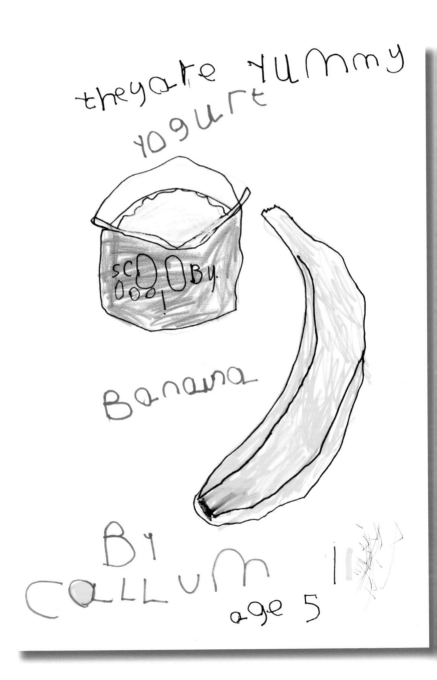

they ate yummy yogurt

Scooby doo!

Banana

By
Callum
age 5

yogurt and honey

Because it is sweet and healthy.

SOME YOGHURT
SOME HONEY
AND MIX

EXOTIC FRUIT SALAD

INGREDIENTS

1 pineapple
5 kiwi fruits
4 oranges
4 peaches
2 tins of mango (natural juices)
1 tub of strawberries
1 bunch of white grapes
1 bunch of red grapes
1 lemon
2 small melons
4 bananas

METHOD

◊   Peel and dice, pineapple, kiwis, oranges, peaches, mango, grapes (de-seeded), melons, strawberries.
◊   Squeeze lemon over fruit and mix around in bowl gently.
◊   Just before serving dice the banana's and add to the fruit salad.
◊   Serve

Exotic Fruit Salad.

Chloe   age 6

I like this because it is scrumpy
and juicy and colourful.

Sammy   and   George's
age 7   age 5

Fresh Fruit Salad

Ingredients: Small portions of:

    Banana
    apple
    pear
    grapes
    or whatever is in season.

    Yogart or Lower fat Cream

1. Peel, deseed and chop fruit required
2. Put in small bowl with a dollop of yogart or lower fat cream.

Tip   more gets eaten if children 'help'!

" We really like this!"

CHARLOTTE'S FRUIT SALAD

Mango, melon, 2 oranges, 1 red apple, 2 kiwi fruit, small bunch of grapes, paw paw, Strawberries, raspberries and any other fruit in season.

Peel mango, melon, paw paw, kiwi fruit and oranges. Cut into chunks removing the inside skin and pith from oranges, wash apple and slice with skin on, cut grapes in half and add strawberries and raspberries. Make a syrup with 2 tabs sugar and boiling water and add juice of a lemon or lime and pour over fruit. Leave for several hours. Serve chilled

AS MUCH AS YOU LIKE
FRUIT SALAD

INGREDIENTS

Apples
Bananas
Strawberries
Grapes

METHOD

◊   Wash the apples, grapes and strawberries and chop them up into small pieces.
◊   Peel and chop the banana. Add to the other fruit and mix around.
◊   Serve with either yoghurt or ice cream.

AS much as you
Like Fruit Salad

I Like Fruit salad
Because I Like Fruit

fruit salad? bannana and orange and grapes and apples and strawberries and cream and shere